For Uche and Ifeyinwa,
without whom this book would not
have been possible

An African Christmas copyright © Frances Lincoln Limited 2005
Text and photographs copyright © Ifeoma Onyefulu 2005
Photograph on page 6 © Mamta Kapoor

The author would like to thank Fuji Ltd for supplying the films.

First published in Great Britain in 2005 by Frances Lincoln Limited,
4 Torriano Mews, Torriano Avenue, London NW5 2RZ
www.franceslincoln.com

Distributed in the USA by Publishers Group West

British Library Cataloguing in Publication Data
available on request

ISBN 1-84507-387-8

Set in Myriad and Today
Printed in China
1 3 5 7 9 8 6 4 2

An African Christmas

Ifeoma Onyefulu

FRANCES LINCOLN CHILDREN'S BOOKS

Introduction

When I was a child in Nigeria, Christmas for me meant new clothes, a church service, presents of money, and watching Mmọ dancing – just like the boy in this book. I was thrilled and also terrified of Mmọ, because to me they looked like monsters with no eyes or mouth, monsters that ran carrying long canes and scattering the crowds.

In Igboland, the part of Nigeria I come from, the word *Mmọ* (pronounced "moor") means "masquerade" or "spirit", the spirit of our ancestors. It has other names in other parts of Africa. Dancing in Mmọ masks and costumes at festival time is a way of remembering our ancestors.

Mmọ are usually men in their twenties or thirties and are often appointed by a council of village elders to perform at a festival. Women are never allowed anywhere near Mmọ. A woman cannot become a Mmọ, but she can watch them perform. As a woman photographer, I am allowed to take photographs of Mmọ, provided I ask permission first and stand at a respectful distance. Mmọ is mysterious, and people like to keep it that way.

A would-be Mmọ goes through some difficult initiation ceremonies before becoming a Mmọ. And real Mmọ are magnificent to behold, with their fantastic colours, their incredible dance movements and the exciting drum rhythms that accompany them.

A F R I C A

Nigeria

"I'm going to be a Mmọ this Christmas. I shall wear a mask over my eyes, my mouth and my face. No one, not even Uncle Ody, will know it's me."

"You can't do that, Afam!" said my sister, Vicky.

"Yes I can," I said. "I love dressing up and I am going to make the most beautiful and colourful Mmọ ever."

Mmọ is not a Christian ritual, but it is part of our Christmas celebrations. Everyone goes back to their villages at Christmas time, so this is when local kings celebrate their achievements with masquerades.

"Have you got a fan, some bits of cloth, a cardboard box, string, a cane and a feather?" asked Vicky.

"No…" I said.

"Do you know how to dance?" Vicky asked.

"Yes, I do!" I said. "I can dance like a Mmọ."

I ran outside. I had to find the things to make my Mmọ beautiful.

Just then, my mum asked me to buy some palm oil and pepper from Mama Ify, to make soup for dinner.

I changed my clothes and went out. When I came back, I found a white feather on the ground. I showed it to Vicky.

"But you still don't have a fan, cloth, cardboard and string," she said.

"I'll get them, Vicky, you'll see."

Then my mum said it was three days to Christmas and a good haircut was what I needed. So I went to the barber's instead.

Vicky had her hair done too. Hers took a very long time.

That afternoon, my dad asked me to count all the soft drinks in the house and put them in the fridge for Christmas.

Then he sent me and my brothers down the road to the tailor, who was making us new clothes for Christmas. And guess what? The tailor gave me lots of pieces of cloth he didn't need!

Later I showed them to Vicky.
"All I need now, Vicky, is a fan,
some string, a cardboard box and
a cane to make the best Mmọ ever."

The next day we went to church. There were lots of people there and it was good to see them all.

When we came back, my mum asked me to buy a box of crackers from Aboki's shop. And guess what? Aboki gave me a cardboard box to make my Mmọ!

I showed the box to Vicky.
"But you still need a fan
and some string," she said.
"Yes, I know, but I want
to start making my Mmọ now."
Vicky came and watched
me cutting out the mask.
But while I was cutting,
my mum and dad told us
we were all going to Awkuzu,
our family's village,
for Christmas.

When we reached Awkuzu, it was Christmas Eve.
There were dancers everywhere. I ran out to watch them.

My mum told me they were the new dancers everyone had been waiting to see. She said they were really special. I thought so, too.

 One of the dancers gave me a fan and some string.
But I *still* hadn't made my Mmọ! I felt so sad.

The next day was Christmas Day.
Everyone was busy cooking and
cleaning.

After we'd finished, we went
to church. I wore my best clothes
and a pair of sunglasses.

My sister Vicky was wearing
a beautiful dress and sunglasses too.
She said I looked as handsome
as Uncle Ody.

Sunglasses are bought by parents
at Christmas-time to make their
children look beautiful, because
everyone wants to look their best.

When we came back, we had a special meal. I ate my favourite food – *chin-chin*, *jellof rice*, salad and fried chicken – and drank Coca-cola. I ate and ate until I thought my stomach was going to burst!

Chin-chin are made from flour, eggs, water and sugar mixed together, then cut into shapes and fried in groundnut oil.

Jellof rice (above) is white rice cooked in tomato sauce.
Top right: My favourite salad
Bottom right: Fried chicken

My friends came to our house, and they were all dressed up for Christmas. My mum and dad gave them some money. But I still couldn't finish my Mmọ, because we all went out again.

There were more dancers in the street –
and Mmọ too! There was a scary Mmọ,
an animal Mmọ and a teenage Mmọ.

Just when the sun was setting, there was a special gun salute to announce the king of Mmọ, *Ijele*! It was the biggest and most beautiful Mmọ ever!

"My Mmọ will be just as beautiful as that," I said, and Vicky smiled.

As soon as we got home, I went on making my mask. I just had one more thing to do.

Ijele Mmọ only appears three or four times a year, and is very special indeed. If a chief or a local king dies, Ijele will appear after three cannons have been fired. It may also appear on Christmas Day and New Year's Day, when a new king is crowned, or at a big festival.

The next day, Uncle Ody came to our house. He is my favourite uncle, and I ran out to say hello to him. Then I ran back and went on making my Mmọ. At last it was finished!

I was so excited. I put it on
and walked slowly out to where
Uncle Ody and everyone could
see me.

Vicky said, "Look, a wonderful,
wonderful Mmọ!"

My brothers played some
music and I danced.

Everyone clapped and clapped. Uncle Ody said the Mmọ was the best he had seen for a long time.

So I danced some more, like a real Mmọ!

Uncle Ody gave the Mmọ – that's me – some money to buy sweets. And I danced and danced until my legs hurt.

Now I can't wait for next Christmas. I shall be an even bigger Mmọ! You'll see.